INSECTS AROUND THE WORLD

ALL ABOUT NORTH AMERICAN YELLOWJACKETS

Annette Whipple

EZ READERS

Creating Young Nonfiction Readers

EZ Readers lets children delve into nonfiction at beginning reading levels. Young readers are introduced to new concepts, facts, ideas, and vocabulary.

Tips for Reading Nonfiction with Beginning Readers

Talk about Nonfiction

Begin by explaining that nonfiction books give us information that is true. The book will be organized around a specific topic or idea, and we may learn new facts through reading.

Look at the Parts

Most nonfiction books have helpful features. Our *EZ Readers* include color photographs and graphic aids, a table of contents, a glossary, and an index. Share the purpose of these features with your reader.

Color Photos and Graphic Aids

A lot of information can be found by "reading" photos, charts, maps, and other graphic aids found within nonfiction texts. Help your reader learn more about the different ways information can be displayed.

Table of Contents

Located at the front of the book, this list shows the big ideas within the text and the page numbers where they can be found.

Glossary

Located at the back of the book, the glossary defines key words and phrases that are related to the topic. These words and phrases can be found in the text in colored type.

Index

Located at the back of the book, an index is an alphabetical list of topics and the page numbers where they can be found.

With a little help and guidance about reading nonfiction, you can feel good about introducing a young reader to the world of *EZ Readers* nonfiction books.

Mitchell Lane
PUBLISHERS

2001 SW 31st Avenue
Hallandale, FL 33009
www.mitchelllane.com

First Edition, 2025.

Author: Annette Whipple
Designer: Rhea Magaro
Editor: Kim Thompson

Names/credits:
Title: All About North American Yellowjackets / by Annette Whipple
Description: Hallandale, FL :
Mitchell Lane Publishers, [2025]

Series: Insects Around the World
Library bound ISBN: 979-8-89260-107-8
eBook ISBN: 978-1-68020-958-7

EZ Readers is an imprint of
Mitchell Lane Publishers

PHOTO CREDITS
Alamy: Monkey Business, 6-7; Dreamstime: Sirbartolini, 20-21; iStock: MiromA, cover, 1; Shutterstock: Paul Reeves Photography, 4-5; Elena11, 8-9; JPL Designs, 10-11; IanRedding, 12-13; Jens Goos, 14-15; Mircea Costina, 16-17; Dmytro Khlystun, 18-19; nblx, 22; JoannaTkaczuk, 22; John_T, 22; Hannamariah, 22

Paperback ISBN: 979-8-89260-145-0

CONTENTS

Yellowjackets are flying **insects**. They look like bees, but they are not bees. They are a kind of wasp. A yellowjacket has yellow stripes around its **abdomen**. It is about the size of a peanut.

Some kinds of yellowjackets live in the ground. Other kinds live in trees or bushes. Some yellowjackets make nests on the sides of buildings. All yellowjackets live in groups called **colonies**. There can be up to 5,000 yellowjackets in a colony.

Only the queen yellowjacket lives through winter. When she wakes up in the spring, she chews plants. She mixes the chewed-up plants with her spit to make a paste. She shapes the paste into a small nest. The nest looks like it is made of brown paper. The queen fills the nest with small **cells**.

The queen yellowjacket lays an egg in each cell. The eggs hatch into **larvae**. The queen feeds them. They grow up to be workers. The workers care for each other. Then the queen lays more eggs.

Yellowjackets eat meat and plants. They use their strong jaws to eat other insects. They like to eat fruit and other sweet foods.

Workers visit many flowers. They eat flower **pollen**. They drink **nectar** from flowers. They collect food for young yellowjackets.

The workers have other jobs too. They feed the new young. They clean the nest and make it bigger. They fan their wings inside the nest. This helps keep the nest warm.

Most of the time, yellowjackets are gentle. But they will protect their nest. If they think a person or animal might harm them, they will sting over and over.

Because yellowjackets sting, many people think they are bad. But they are very helpful. They eat insect **pests** that destroy farm crops. They also **pollinate** plants. This lets the plants make seeds so more plants can grow. Yellowjackets pollinate plants that make food for people. We need yellowjackets.

WHERE DO YELLOWJACKETS LIVE?

Yellowjackets live all over North America. You can find them in these habitats.

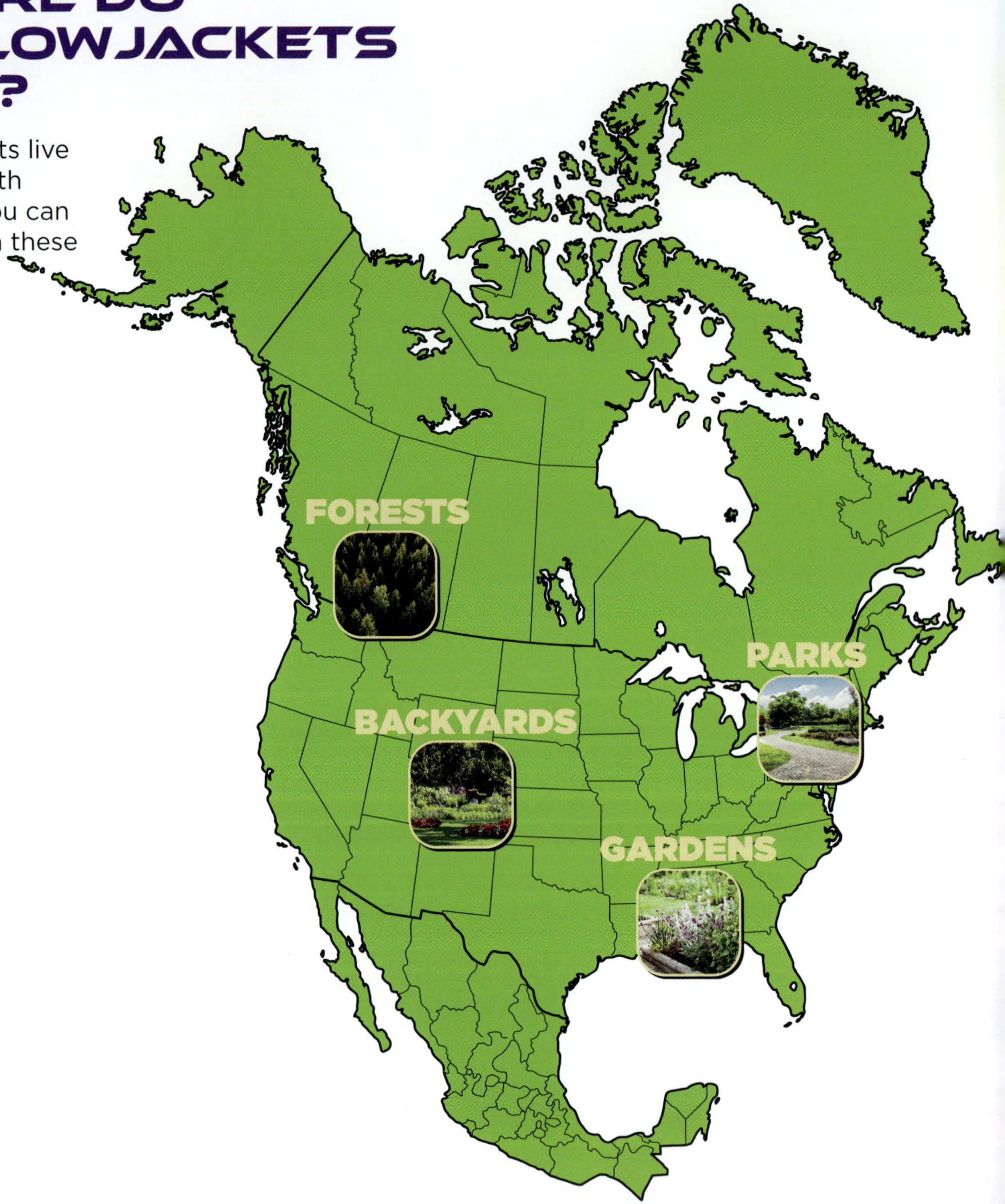

INTERESTING FACTS

- Male yellowjackets do not have stingers and die after mating.
- Female workers die when it gets too cold.
- Yellowjacket larvae look like maggots.
- Yellowjackets like the sweetness of soda.
- The bald-face hornet is a yellowjacket, not a hornet.

PARTS OF A YELLOWJACKET

Antennae
Antennae are the feelers on a yellowjacket's head that help it sense and understand the world.

Eyes
Seeing well helps yellowjackets find food.

Mandibles
Strong jaws, called mandibles, help yellowjackets catch and eat insects.

Stinger
The stinger on a female yellowjacket's abdomen helps her protect herself and the nest.

Tongue
A yellowjacket's tongue is the perfect shape for sipping flower nectar and fruit juice.

GLOSSARY

abdomen (AB-duh-muhn)
The rear part of an insect's body

cells (sels)
Small rooms

colonies (KAH-luh-neez)
Large groups of animals that live together

insects (IN-sekts)
Small animals with hard outer skeletons, six legs, and three body sections

larvae (LAHR-vee)
Young insects after they hatch; the stage of life when an insect looks like a worm

nectar (NEK-tur)
A sweet liquid made by flowers

pests (pests)
Insects or other animals that cause destruction and damage, especially on farms

pollen (PAH-luhn)
Powder made by flowers to help them reproduce

pollinate (PAH-luh-nate)
To spread pollen from flower to flower, which helps plants reproduce

INDEX

FURTHER READING

Harvey, Sarah. *Wasps: Backyard Bugs and Creepy-Crawlies*. Oliver, British Columbia, Canada: Engage Books, 2022.

Zimmerman, Adeline J. *Bee or Wasp?* Minnesota, MN: Jump, Inc., 2022.

ON THE INTERNET

Ducksters: Yellowjacket Wasp
https://www.ducksters.com/animals/yellow_jacket_wasp.php
Get your big questions about yellowjackets answered at this fun site.

Meet the Meat Bee...The Western Yellowjacket!
https://www.youtube.com/watch?v=yF61-E-Jq20
Watch a yellowjacket visit a backyard picnic and return to the colony to feed the young.